LOVE ON 18 WHEELS

Navigating Marriage and the Open Road

ROBERT & SHARON PORTER

Movement with Precision Publishing

Love on 18 Wheels –
Navigating Marriage and the Open Road
Copyright © 2025 by Robert & Sharon Porter
All rights reserved.

Published by Movement with
Precision Publishing Orangeburg, SC

This is a work of nonfiction. Unless otherwise indicated, all names, characters, businesses, places, events, and incidents are the product of the author's direct experience or used with permission. Any resemblance to actual persons, living or dead, or actual events is purely coincidental or used illustratively.

Library of Congress Control Number:
Application submitted and number pending.
ISBN: 978-1-967964-00-0

For information, contact:
hello@loveon18wheels.com

First Edition: May 2025
Printed in the United States of America

DEDICATION

To every married trucking couple out there—whether you just tied the knot or have been rolling together for decades—this book is for you.

To the newlyweds navigating love and logistics, learning each other's rhythms between weigh stations and windshield time—we see you.

To the seasoned couples who've weathered storms, breakdowns, and broker drama but still choose each other every day—you inspire us.

To the ones who aren't in a truck but want to learn how to build a marriage that lasts—this isn't just about the road. It's about the ride of life. And we hope these lessons help you grow in patience, purpose, and partnership, wherever your journey leads.

And to the singles preparing for marriage, wondering how to find the right person and how to be the right person—this book is for you too. Marriage is less about perfect compatibility and more about shared commitment, trust, and grace. Whether you're riding in a semi or simply walking through life side-by-side, the principles are the same: love, lead, serve, and laugh often.

This book is a tribute to the real, raw, beautiful work of partnership.

We're honored to share the journey with you.

See you down the road.

Acknowledgements

First and foremost, we give all glory and honor to God.

We didn't volunteer to go back on the road—but the Lord had other plans. This wasn't just a return to trucking. It was an invitation into a divine classroom. Through every mountain pass and midnight haul, God was teaching us. Strengthening us. Humbling us. Showing us how to love better, trust deeper, and walk in unity—not just with each other, but with Him.

The cab of that truck became a sanctuary. A place where we prayed through breakdowns, mediated through conflicts, and found peace in the middle of chaos. It was our rolling classroom, our place of transformation. Every mile was a lesson. Every challenge was a chance to grow. Every quiet hour behind the wheel was a call to draw closer to the One who called us.

This book, this life, this journey—it's all because of His grace and guidance. We are grateful beyond words.

TABLE OF CONTENTS

INTRODUCTION

LIFE IN THE FAST LANE

———————⦾⦾⦾⦾———————

Life as a trucking couple isn't for the faint of heart. It's an adventure, a partnership, and occasionally, a test of who can hold their tongue the longest when the GPS reroutes you down a questionable dirt road. It's waking up in a different state every morning, navigating tight docks and even tighter schedules, and sharing a living space so small that there's no room for silent treatment (or slamming doors). It's learning to love each other through traffic jams, late-night runs, and the occasional wrong turn (which, let's be honest, is never our fault, right?).

For those of us who have chosen to take on this wild life together, we know that trucking isn't just a job—it's a lifestyle, a business, and a 24/7 crash course in patience, communication, and love all rolled into one. It's not just about getting freight from Point A to Point B; it's about navigating the road of life together. You learn to argue without scaring the four-wheelers, and mastering the art of teamwork—not just to keep the wheels turning, but to keep the relationship strong.

Most people can't imagine spending nearly every waking hour with their spouse, let alone working with them. But for those of us who call the cab home, marriage isn't just about love—it's about partnership, resilience, and learning how to back each other up, literally and figuratively.

But here's the thing: Trucking together can be one of the most rewarding experiences in a marriage. It teaches you patience, strengthens your communication, and forces you to rely on each other in a way that few other professions do.

Every trucking couple quickly realizes that the key to success isn't just love—it's teamwork. You're not just life partners; you're co-drivers, business partners, and problem solvers navigating tight spaces and even tighter deadlines.

♦ Marriage on the Move – How do you keep the romance alive when your "date nights" involve truck stop buffets and your arguments happen at 70 mph? (Hint: communication, patience, and sometimes just letting the other person win.)

- Divide and Conquer – Figuring out who does what makes life smoother, whether it's handling the paperwork, booking loads, or making sure someone always remembers the snacks.

- Mind Over Miles – Some days, the road is long, the dispatcher is frustrating, and the load is heavy—emotionally and physically. How do you lift each other up when the miles feel endless?

- Business Partners in Love – Your relationship isn't just romantic; it's an enterprise. Goal-setting, financial planning, and keeping emotions in check during stressful runs are all part of the journey.

- Handling Disagreements in a Small Space – There's no storming off to another room when your house is 8 feet wide. Conflict resolution is key, and sometimes, laughter is the best peace offering.

- Covering for Each Other – Everyone has strengths and weaknesses. Success comes from knowing when to lead, when to follow, and when to just hand your partner a snack and let them drive.

- Avoiding Rivalry and Resentment – Keeping score in a marriage (or on the road) leads to nothing but potholes. The only competition should be against the GPS arrival time.

♦ Staying Healthy Together – Sleep, nutrition, and sanity checks aren't optional when you're running a two-person operation. Keeping each other accountable makes all the difference.

♦ Laughing Through the Lanes – If you don't laugh about the crazy stuff that happens on the road, you'll cry. Finding joy in the journey is what makes the miles worth it.

♦ Reflecting on the Road Behind and the Journey Ahead – What has trucking taught us about love, life, and each other? More than we ever expected.

What This Book Will Give You

This isn't just a guide—it's a roadmap for trucking couples who want to make their marriage as strong as their business. Whether you're new to team driving or seasoned pros looking for fresh perspective, you'll find:

♦ Real-life stories from the road (including lessons learned the hard way).

♦ Practical tips on balancing love and logistics.

♦ Humor—because if you can't laugh at trucking life, you won't survive it.

Our goal is simple: to help you navigate marriage and the open road without losing your mind—or each other.

So, fasten your seatbelts, keep your eyes on the road, and get ready to roll. The journey of a lifetime isn't just about the miles you cover—it's about who you're sharing them with.

CHAPTER 1

TWO HEARTS, ONE CAB – MARRIAGE ON THE MOVE

———⊰⊱———

The hum of the engine, the rhythmic sound of tires against the road, and the ever-changing scenery outside the windshield—this is our version of home. Most couples build their marriage in a house with four walls, a backyard, and maybe a picket fence. For us, love lives on 18 wheels.

Living and working together in a space no bigger than a walk-in closet isn't for the faint of heart. It requires patience, teamwork, and the ability to laugh when things go sideways—literally and figuratively. Sharing a cab means there's nowhere to storm off to after an argument, no "I'll just go sleep on the couch" option, and certainly no silent treatments that last beyond the next truck stop.

Or threatening to put your spouse out on the catwalk with a bungee cord and driving faster. In this chapter, we'll explore what it takes to keep a marriage strong while navigating the open road together.

What Does It Take to Keep a Marriage Strong While Navigating the Open Road?

Let's be real—being married is already a full-time job. Now imagine adding another full-time job on top of that... *with the same person.* There are no breaks, no commutes to separate offices, no "how was your day?" recaps over dinner because, well, you *lived* each other's day minute by minute. This is where you need to establish your personal boundaries. So, you can clear your head for the next load that you will take on. This is important for your safety and judgment while rolling on 18 wheels.

And yet, when it works, it's magic.

Tip: When things get stressful, allow each other space to work it out within yourself individually first, then come together and communicate the issue at hand. Small adjustments can make a big difference.

It takes **intentional communication**—not just about who's driving next or what exit to take, but about feelings, frustrations, and fears. We've learned that small issues become big ones fast when you're trapped together in a rolling metal box. So we check in with each other regularly, not just about the route, but about how we're doing mentally and emotionally. "You good?" might be the most powerful two-word marriage saver on the road.

It takes **laughter**, especially when things go wrong. Like the time we got directions from the receiver to bring a load of ice cream into San Francisco, CA. The woman gave us the wrong directions and we ended up on a road that was so steep like in the movies you literally seen cars bounce off the road as they were coming down it. We started up the hill which seems like it took forever to get up. We won't name names again but one of us wanted to get out of the truck and walk up because it was so frightening. By the time we got to the top, we had about a mile-long of cars behind us. Once the road opened up and cars could pass, we were blessed with fingers, sign language, and nicknames that we would not repeat to a child. We've learned that if you don't laugh about it, you'll probably cry—or worse, argue over whose fault it was until the next weigh station.

It takes **respecting each other's rhythm**. Just because you're in the same space doesn't mean you're always in the same headspace. Sometimes, one of us needs silence, while the other needs a good playlist and conversation. Finding a balance between alone time and together time in a cab takes practice, like learning each other's boundaries.

It takes **teamwork**—real, tag-you're-it, I-got-your-back-no-matter-what teamwork. When one of us is exhausted, the other steps up. When one makes a mistake, the other doesn't keep score. We don't always agree on the best route or the best way to back into a tight dock, but we've learned to trust that we both want the same thing: to make it through safely and sanely, together.

And above all, it takes **commitment**. Not just to each other, but to the shared calling that got us into that cab in the first place. We're not just hauling freight—we're building a life. One mile, one load, one adventure at a time.

Keeping the Romance Alive (Despite the Noise)

Between the constant hum of the road, the bouncing off the bed from the bumps in the road that throw you two inches in the air, and the occasional angry motorist yelling at you for simply existing, romance isn't always the first thing on a trucker couple's mind. But if you're not intentional about nurturing your relationship, it's easy to slip into a routine where you become more business partners than life partners. You must always keep in mind that your marriage comes first before the business.

Ways to Keep the Spark Alive:

- ♦ Date Nights on the Road – Whether it's stopping at a scenic overlook for a picnic or watching the sunset from a truck stop diner, find small ways to create special moments.

♦ Love Notes & Surprise Treats – A sticky note on the dashboard, a surprise snack from the last stop, or even a simple "thinking of you" text can go a long way.

♦ Music & Memories – Create playlists that remind you of special moments together. Playing "your song" while cruising down the highway can make even the longest stretch of road feel romantic.

♦ Kissing each other before switching drivers – Don't underestimate the power of a simple kiss. A kiss can remind you why you're in this together.

Fighting Fair: Disagreements at 70 MPH

Let's be honest—arguments happen in every marriage. But when your home is on wheels, resolving conflicts quickly becomes a necessity. There's no slamming doors or taking a walk to cool off. Instead, you learn to handle disagreements with maturity, humor, and efficiency.

Rules for Conflict Resolution in a Truck:

1. No Fighting While One Person Is Driving – The road requires focus, and heated arguments can be

dangerous. If tensions rise, agree to pause the discussion until a safe time.

2. Use "We" Instead of "You" – Saying "We need to figure this out" instead of "You always do this" makes a huge difference in how a conversation unfolds.

3. Don't play the blame game and hold grudges – Holding grudges in a small space is like letting a skunk loose in the cab—unpleasant for everyone involved. If you're wrong, own it.

4. Find the Humor – Sometimes, the best way to defuse a disagreement is to laugh at how ridiculous it is. Arguments divides the team.

5. Have a Reset Button – Whether it's a moment of silence or taking a deep breath, find a way to signal when it's time to move forward and let go of the argument.

The Strength of Love on 18 Wheels

Marriage is a journey, and for couples who call the highway home, that journey comes with unique challenges—but also incredible rewards. There's something special about sharing the road with your best friend, navigating life's twists and turns together, and knowing that no matter where you park for the night, you're always home as long as you have each other.

At the end of the day, love on 18 wheels isn't about the size of the space—it's about the strength of the bond.

And if two people can make a home out of a moving vehicle, there's nothing they can't handle together.

Final Thoughts

Marriage on the move isn't about perfection—it's about partnership. It's about learning to love someone not just when they're at their best, but when they've gone three days without a real shower and can't remember where they left their flip-flop (spoiler: the bed ate them).

It's about seeing the country through the same windshield, chasing sunsets and fuel stops and shared goals, knowing that no matter what direction the road takes you, you've got someone riding shotgun who makes the journey worthwhile.

In the end, love doesn't need four walls to grow. Sometimes, all it needs is a little diesel, a lot of patience, and someone who's willing to ride with you—through traffic jams, blown tires, and every beautiful mile in between.

CHAPTER 2

DIVIDE AND CONQUER – KNOWING YOUR ROLES

Trucking as a couple is a lot like dancing—you both need to know your steps, stay in sync, and avoid stepping on each other's toes. Without clear roles, it's easy to trip over each other, leading to frustration, inefficiency, and the occasional "Why didn't you just let me handle it?" moment.

In the world of team trucking, success depends on two things: defining responsibilities and trusting your partner to handle their part of the load. Whether it's who drives which shifts, who handles paperwork, or who deals with maintenance, having clear roles can mean the difference between a smooth ride and a rocky road.

Who Does What? Defining Clear Roles

One of the biggest mistakes trucking couples make is assuming that roles will just naturally fall into place. Spoiler alert: they don't. Without a clear plan, you'll find yourselves constantly stepping on each other's tasks—or worse, assuming the other person will handle something that gets forgotten altogether. (Like that time we both thought the other had taken the lock of the loaded trailer before leaving the receiver. Let's just say buying another lock became a priority.)

Common Roles in a Trucking Team:

1. The Driver (Primary & Secondary) – Sure, you both drive, but that doesn't mean you drive the same. One might thrive on early morning sunrises and black coffee, while the other doesn't speak human until afternoon. Some prefer night runs for the quiet roads and fewer four-wheelers. Decide who drives what shift, and unless there's a reason to switch, stick with it. Your sanity depends on it.

2. The Trip Planner – Google Maps is nice, but it won't tell you if your truck will get stuck under an 11'6" bridge in upstate New York. Whoever is the research wizard—checking for low bridges, fuel stops, weigh stations, and weather

alerts—should take the lead here. Always plan the trip ahead of time and discuss the route.

3. The Business Manager – This includes managing receipts, invoices, taxes, insurance, permits, and if you're an owner-operator, tracking revenue and expenses. This is the person who makes sure the IRS doesn't come knocking while you're rolling.

4. The Maintenance Coordinator – This person keeps track of oil changes, tire tread, DEF fluid, and the "What's that noise?" checklist. Basically, they make sure your second home doesn't turn into a 40-ton lawn ornament on the side of the road.

5. The Load Negotiator – Especially for owner-ops, someone needs to stay in contact with brokers or dispatchers. They ask the tough questions like, "Is this a live load or drop-and-hook?" and "Is there parking at the receiver, or should we find a truck stop nearby?

Playing to Your Strengths (and Owning Your Weaknesses)

The magic of a good team isn't about doing the same things equally well—it's about balancing each other out. If you're the type who thrives under pressure and loves crunching numbers, the business manager role might be a natural fit. If your partner is a mechanical whiz and gets oddly excited about air filters and fuel injectors, let them run the maintenance department.

What matters most is respecting each other's strengths and trusting each other's judgment. No micro-managing. Once a task is assigned, let that person handle it. If they need help, they'll ask. (Eventually.)

And for the record—owning your weaknesses isn't a flaw. It's actually one of the biggest signs of maturity on the road. If you hate paperwork and your partner has color-coded spreadsheets for fun, guess what? Let them have it. Meanwhile, maybe you're the one who's better at handling unexpected challenges on the road—like navigating a detour without needing therapy afterward.

Communication Is the Grease in the Gears

Dividing roles is only part of the puzzle. Communicating about them is the rest. You might have the best system in the world, but if you don't check in regularly, it's easy to get out of sync.

Pro tip: Have a quick "cab meeting" at least once every new trip. It doesn't have to be formal—just a check-in while waiting on a dock or eating dinner. Go over the upcoming week: routes, deadlines, upcoming maintenance, finances, anything lingering that hasn't been addressed.

And if one person is feeling overwhelmed? Talk about it. Roles aren't carved in stone—they can evolve. If someone's carrying more than their fair share, redistribute before burnout becomes a breakdown (in more ways than one).

When Roles Overlap (Or No One Wants the Job)

There are some tasks that nobody *wants* to do—scanning receipts, scrubbing bug guts off the windshield, dealing with cranky dispatchers at 6 a.m. And sometimes, your defined roles get blurry—like when a tire blows and the "maintenance person" is asleep in the back. That's where teamwork kicks in.

If both of you can step up when needed—without playing the blame game—your team becomes unstoppable. It's not about whose job it is at that moment; it's about what needs to be done.

We like to think of these tasks as "floater duties"—the stuff that rotates based on energy, time, or who is up at the time.

Emergencies and Role-Swapping

Sometimes life on the road throws a curveball that forces you to step out of your usual role. Maybe one of you gets sick, or the weather delays your carefully planned schedule, or something as simple as exhaustion means you need to take over for your partner unexpectedly.

That's why cross-training is essential. Even if one of you is the primary trip planner or business brain, the other should have a basic understanding of the process. You don't need to be a pro, but you should be able to fill in during an emergency without having a meltdown or needing a whiteboard and a PowerPoint presentation.

Real-Life Example: The "We'll Just Wing It" Disaster

Years ago in our career, we didn't know how to fuel the truck since we were new owner-operators. We would fill up the truck and be on our way. Then we received our fuel report that showed how much we were paying in fuel taxes. We also didn't know the sweet spot in our truck on how fast we should run for the best fuel mileage.

From that day forward, after speaking with our fuel department, we learned which states to fuel in to maximize our fuel tax credit and discovered the optimal speed for the truck to maximize fuel usage. We sat down and divided responsibilities. We agreed on who handled what, and we checked in every few days to make sure we were both on the same page. The change was instant: fewer arguments, more efficiency, and a lot more laughter.

The Mental Load: The Role No One Talks About

One often overlooked area of roles is the mental and emotional load. Long-haul trucking is stressful, isolating, and physically demanding. Someone has to be the emotional thermostat in the truck—keeping the vibe calm when things get tense, offering encouragement during rough days, and knowing when to crack a joke or give space.

This role shifts based on energy and circumstances. If your partner is having a rough day, step into that supportive role without being asked. Offer the last snack. Queue up their favorite playlist. And when it's your turn to vent or crumble a little? Let them return the favor.

Being each other's emotional support isn't about always being cheerful—it's about being present and patient, even when the reefer is screaming and the clock is ticking.

Renegotiating Roles as Life Changes

Here's the thing about roles: they're fluid. What worked six months ago might not work now. Life changes. Energy levels shift. Maybe one of you starts taking classes online, or you bring a dog on board (hello, new poop patrol duties), or your business evolves.

Check in and renegotiate your roles as needed. Maybe you trade off trip planning every week, or the business manager steps back a bit during tax season to avoid combusting. As long as you keep talking and adjusting, your partner can grow with you—not against you.

Final Thoughts: Two Seats, One Mission

When you're in a relationship where your office, bedroom, kitchen, and entire life are on wheels, clarity is everything. Defining roles isn't about controlling each other—it's about respecting each other's strengths, reducing stress, and running your business and life like a well-oiled machine.

Divide and conquer doesn't mean separating—it means uniting with strategy. It's saying, "I trust you to take the wheel, the phone, the wrench, or the spreadsheet," and knowing they'll do the same when the time comes.

So decide who does what, check in often, stay flexible, and remember: no matter what roles you take on, you're in this together. Two drivers. One truck. One team.

CHAPTER 3

DRIVING EACH OTHER –
MIND OVER MILES

Mind Over Miles – Mental, Emotional, and Spiritual Strength on the Road

When the road stretches endlessly ahead and life feels like one giant detour, it's not just your truck that needs fuel—it's your mindset. *Mind Over Miles* dives into the emotional resilience, spiritual connection, and mental clarity that trucking couples must cultivate to keep rolling strong together.

This chapter is about more than staying motivated. It's about anchoring each other in faith when burnout hits, offering emotional support when the silence gets heavy, and laughing through the chaos when everything seems to be going wrong. From gratitude practices to spiritual check-ins, you'll discover real-life tools and routines that help you build a mindset that isn't just about surviving the road—but thriving on it.

Because when you're driving with your mind right and your heart in sync with your partner's, no load feels too heavy—and every mile brings you closer, not just to your destination, but to each other.

The Power of Mindset: Keeping Your Mental Wheels Aligned

The road can be unpredictable, but one thing you *can* control is your attitude. A positive mindset won't magically clear up traffic jams, fix a busted air hose, or make the GPS stop rerouting you through goat trails—but it *will* change how you respond to those frustrations. And that, right there, is what separates teams who survive from those who thrive.

We've had days when nothing went right—shipper delayed us five hours, the receiver was rude, the weather turned sour, and we were both running on caffeine and fumes. But in the middle of that chaos, a shared laugh or a shift in perspective saved the day.

Growth vs. Fixed Mindset on the Road

A fixed mindset on the road sounds like:

- ◆ "Why does this always happen to us?"
- ◆ "We'll never get ahead in this industry."

- "If we had better luck, we wouldn't be stuck here."

Sound familiar? We've all been there. But that mindset becomes a mental pothole—it wears you out and wrecks your alignment, mentally and emotionally.

In contrast, a *growth mindset* says:

- "Maybe this delay is a divine delay—keeping us from something worse."
- "We've overcome worse. This is just another bump."
- "What can we learn from this situation?"

That mental shift doesn't just reduce stress; it builds trust and cooperation. When you both commit to a growth mindset, even the worst days become learning opportunities. You stop blaming each other or outside circumstances and start solving problems together—like a pit crew working in sync.

Practical Ways to Keep a Positive Mindset

Staying positive isn't automatic—it's a discipline. It's something you build like muscle memory. Here are some daily habits we use that help us stay mentally strong and emotionally steady:

- Morning Mindset Check: Before that first sip of coffee, set your intention for the day. Pray, meditate, listen to something inspiring—or just tell each other, "Let's have a good one today."

♦ Gratitude Over Grumbling: When one of us starts griping, the other will say, "Okay, tell me three things you're grateful for." It's annoying at first—but it works.

♦ Laugh Often and Loud: We've had some silly inside jokes that saved our sanity on 1200-mile days. Laughter is the grease in the gears of your relationship.

♦ Change the Frame: Instead of "Why us?" ask "What now?" Adjust your mindset like you'd adjust your mirrors—often and intentionally.

♦ Visualize Your Goals: Keep a shared vision board in the cab. Pictures of your dream house, financial goals, future vacations—reminders of *why* you're doing this can fuel motivation during rough patches.

When One of You Feels Like Giving Up

There *will* be days when one of you feels like quitting—usually while stuck in traffic with three hours left on the clock and nowhere to park. Maybe one of you is homesick. Maybe burnout is hitting hard. That's when the other partner becomes the lifeline.

Signs One of You Needs Support:

♦ Silence when they're usually chatty

- Snapping over little things
- Withdrawal or lack of enthusiasm
- Saying things like "I don't know if I can do this anymore"

What you can do:

- A sincere "I see you. I appreciate you."
- Remind them why you started this journey together. Financial freedom, independence, or just the love of the road—revisit your "why."
- Acknowledge wins, no matter how small: "You nailed that 90-degree alley dock. I'm still impressed."
- Take something off their plate—literally or figuratively. Let them rest while you handle pre-trip. Offer to drive an extra hour. Make their favorite snack magically appear (or stop at that one place they love).

We've had times where one of us just hit a wall. Instead of pushing harder, we hit pause. Sometimes the best support you can give is rest and reassurance.

Interceding for Each Other: Emotional and Spiritual Support

This job will test your faith, your patience, and your connection—not just to each other, but to something greater. The solitude of the road can be peaceful... or it can feel like a desert. That's why emotional and spiritual support matter so much.

Emotional Support: Listening With Intention

Being emotionally available doesn't mean being a therapist—but it does mean being *present*. Really present.

- ◆ Listen Without Fixing: When your partner vents, don't jump to solutions. Just *listen*. Let them unload without feeling judged or corrected.

- ◆ Know Their Stress Signals: Some people talk more when they're stressed. Others go quiet. Learn your partner's patterns so you can respond with empathy, not frustration.

- ◆ Encourage Breaks: If your spouse is grinding themselves down, speak up. Advocate for a break—even if it's just an extra hour of sleep or a longer meal stop.

Sometimes, we tag in for each other without even asking. If one of us is clearly drained, the other picks up the slack. That kind of mutual awareness and care builds unshakable trust.

Spiritual Support: Faith That Fuels the Journey

For us, faith is the glue that holds it all together. When the miles are long and the days are hard, we lean into prayer, scripture, and shared spiritual practices.

Ideas to stay spiritually connected:

◆ Pray Before You Roll: Even a quick prayer sets the tone for the day and helps you feel united.

◆ Share Devotionals: Listen to a short devotional together during the drive or before bed. It feeds the spirit and gives you something meaningful to reflect on and to discuss.

◆ Accountability With Grace: Help each other grow without criticism. Remind each other to be kind, to have patience—even when someone cuts you off and brake-checks a fully loaded trailer.

Faith on the road doesn't have to be complicated. It just has to be consistent.

Final Thoughts: A Road Worth Traveling Together

Mind Over Miles aren't solo acts—they're a duet. In a trucking marriage, both partners must commit to encouraging each other, staying mentally strong, and offering emotional and spiritual backup when the going gets tough.

You *will* face challenges. Flat tires, foul moods, faulty GPS, and fast food fatigue—it's all part of the lifestyle. But you'll also have front-row seats to sunsets most people never see, quiet nights under starlit skies, and a bond that's forged in diesel, determination, and daily grace.

So, take care of each other. Stay mentally sharp, spiritually grounded, and emotionally connected. Because at the end of the day, you're not just driving freight—you're driving a future. Together.

CHAPTER 4

TEAMWORK MAKES THE DREAM WORK – WORKING AS BUSINESS PARTNERS

Trucking as a couple isn't just about love—it's about business. Whether you're running your own authority, leasing onto a carrier, or company driving as a team, treating your trucking venture like a business is essential to long-term success.

Being married to your business partner comes with unique challenges. You have to make financial decisions together, plan for the future, and stay aligned without letting personal emotions get in the way. That means separating your roles as husband and wife from your roles as business partners—because nothing kills romance faster than arguing over fuel costs during date night.

In this chapter, we'll talk about how to approach trucking as a business, set clear goals, and make sound decisions together while keeping your relationship strong.

Running Your Truck Like a Business

Many trucking couples fall into the trap of treating their work like "just a job" instead of a business. But the truth is, whether you're an owner-operator or a company driver, your truck is your business. The more professionally you approach it, the more successful you'll be.

Business Mindset vs. Employee Mindset

An **employee mindset** focuses on:

- ♦ Just getting the job done and collecting a paycheck.
- ♦ Reacting to problems instead of planning ahead.
- ♦ Blaming external circumstances instead of taking control.

A **business mindset** focuses on:

- ♦ Making strategic decisions that maximize profit.

- Planning for expenses, maintenance, and financial growth.
- Taking responsibility for success rather than relying on luck.

If you're driving as a team, you're not just co-drivers—you're co-owners of your trucking venture. The decisions you make together impact your finances, your schedule, and your future. Treat it seriously, and it will reward you.

Setting Goals Together: Financial, Professional, and Personal

Every business needs a roadmap, and every couple needs a shared vision. That's why setting goals together is crucial. Without a clear destination, you'll just be spinning your wheels—moving, but not making real progress.

Financial Goals: Planning for Profit and Freedom

Money can be a major stressor in any relationship, but when you're in business together, it's even more important to be on the same page financially. Sit down and ask yourselves:

- What's our ideal income per year?
- How much do we want to save for retirement?
- What's our plan for paying off debts?

♦ How can we maximize profits while reducing expenses?

Clear financial goals guide your day-to-day decisions: whether to take a particular load, when to invest in equipment, or how to budget for the unexpected.

Real Talk: When Life Hits the Fan

We've been there.

We had just come off a solid run when our truck engine gave out—completely. Just like that, we were out of commission. There's nothing like the sound of your livelihood going silent on the side of the road. It was a hard blow—not just financially, but mentally and emotionally too.

We had to make a quick decision, and fast. We ended up working under another business owner within the same company. At the time, it seemed like the best option—keep moving, keep earning, stay afloat. But after a while, we knew deep down: this arrangement wasn't sustainable. We didn't share the same values, and the longer we stayed, the harder it would be to get back into our own truck.

We prayed—seriously prayed—for wisdom and clarity. We knew our goal: get back into our own truck, but we had to work together to make it happen. That meant restructuring our finances, cutting unnecessary expenses, and focusing every effort on saving for a new down payment.

There were sacrifices—fewer takeout meals, less shopping, no unnecessary expenses. We had to hustle smart, plan everything out, and stay united even when it was stressful. But several months later, we did it. We bought another truck and got back to doing what we loved—on our own terms.

Without setting that goal and pulling together, we'd still be stuck working someone else's plan. That experience reminded us: teamwork and clear vision are everything.

Professional Goals: Growing Your Business and Skills

Beyond just keeping the wheels turning, what do you want to achieve professionally?

- Do you want to become owner-operators if you're not already?
- Start a small fleet?
- Transition into training or mentoring other couples?
- Take specialized freight that pays more but requires certifications?

These are big-picture questions that help shape the direction of your business. Maybe you want to eventually move off the road and manage things from home. Maybe you want to diversify with investments, logistics, or even writing a book (hey, you're reading one now, right?).

Whatever your aspirations are, keep them visible and revisit them often. Let your business evolve with your vision—not just out of necessity.

Personal Goals: Keeping Your Relationship Strong

Let's not forget that you're more than business partners. You're spouses, lovers, best friends (and sometimes unwilling bunkmates when someone forgets to shower). Personal goals matter too.

- ◆ **Health & Wellness**: Long hauls and fast food can take a toll. Make time for walking, stretching, or prepping healthy meals.
- ◆ **Quality Time**: Even when you're in the truck together, quality time can fall by the wayside. Plan date nights—even if it's just watching a show together parked at a truck stop.
- ◆ **Rest**: Running too hard too long is a recipe for burnout. Rest is not a luxury—it's fuel for your relationship and your business.

When your personal and business goals are in harmony, you won't just survive out here—you'll thrive.

Making Business Decisions Without Letting Emotions Take Over

Mixing marriage and money can be like playing with fire and gasoline if you're not careful. It's so easy to let personal feelings cloud professional judgment. But being able to communicate calmly and make logical decisions is a skill worth building.

Common Emotional Traps (and How to Dodge Them)

1. **The "Who's Right?" Debate**
   - Business decisions aren't about winning arguments. They're about solving problems.
   - Instead of, "I told you so," try "Let's figure this out together."

2. **Fear-Driven Decisions**
   - Fear of taking a risk can keep you stuck.
   - Don't let fear make choices for you. Use facts, not feelings.

3. **Personal Disagreements Bleeding Into Business**
   - If you're mad that your spouse forgot your anniversary, maybe now's not the time to discuss maintenance budgets.
   - Take time to separate emotional moments from business meetings.

How to Make Better Decisions Together

- ◆ Have a regular "business meeting" once a week. Talk money, loads, maintenance, and goals.
- ◆ Use a shared decision-making process:
  1. Define the problem.
  2. Gather facts.
  3. List pros and cons.
  4. Decide together.
- ◆ Let each partner lead in their strength zone. If one of you is better with numbers, let them handle the budget. If the other's great with dispatch or communication, give them that task.

You're not adversaries—you're allies. Don't let your ego drive the truck.

Final Thoughts: Driving Toward Success Together

Running a trucking business as a married couple is not for the faint of heart. It takes grit, communication, grace, and a whole lot of patience. But when you get it right, it's one of the most rewarding journeys you can take.

Treat your trucking like a real business. Set clear goals—financial, professional, and personal. Make decisions from logic, not emotions. Work together, pray together, and never lose sight of the bigger picture.

You'll face breakdowns—both mechanical and emotional—but you'll also have breakthroughs. You'll argue, laugh, cry, and grow. And through it all, you'll become not just better business owners, but stronger partners in life.

Because in the end, it's not just the miles that matter—it's who's riding beside you.

CHAPTER 5

CAB CONFLICTS – HANDLING DISAGREEMENTS ON THE ROAD

When you share an office, a bedroom, a kitchen, and a living room—all within the confines of a truck cab—disagreements are inevitable. Unlike a traditional home, where you can storm off to another room or go for a solo drive to cool down, a trucking couple has nowhere to escape. The cab is both your workplace and your home, which means grudges have nowhere to hide—and tension can build fast if conflicts aren't handled properly.

But here's the truth: a little conflict isn't a bad thing. In fact, it's normal. The key isn't avoiding disagreements—it's knowing how to work through them quickly, effectively, and with as little damage as possible (to each other or to the truck).

This chapter is all about learning to resolve conflicts in a way that strengthens your relationship rather than wears it down. From practical techniques to using humor as a secret weapon, let's dive into keeping your marriage smooth, even when the road gets bumpy.

Why the Cab Is No Place for Grudges

Holding a grudge in a house is one thing. Holding a grudge in a 70-square-foot space on wheels? That's a recipe for disaster.

Unlike couples who work separate jobs and come home to vent to a friend or unwind alone, trucking couples don't get a break from each other. That's why it's so important to address conflicts early—before resentment has a chance to build.

Here's what happens when you let a disagreement fester in the truck:

- The silent treatment turns into an awkward, miserable ride.
- Small annoyances suddenly feel 10 times bigger.
- Tension makes the job harder and more dangerous.

♦ One person eventually explodes (or worse—takes it out on dispatch).

We had a perfect example of this not too long ago. One of us booked a load that seemed alright at first glance. The rate looked okay, the timing worked, and we wanted to keep moving. But once we were locked in and rolling, it became painfully obvious—it wasn't worth the time or the money. It was short, paid low, and left us stuck without anything decent on the back end.

Frustration kicked in quick. The other person was irritated (and rightly so) and made it known. But we were already committed, and there was no backing out.

The silence in the cab was louder than engine noise. We tried to find another load going in the direction we needed to go, just to help cover fuel. It took all day, and the best we could find was a short, cheap run—less than 400 miles and barely worth the effort. Talk about a mood.

Eventually, the one who booked the load owned up to it: "That one's on me. I messed up." And just like that, the wall started to come down.

That moment could've easily turned into an all-day argument, but what saved us was humility, quick forgiveness, and the decision not to let it linger. We talked it out, chalked it up as a lesson learned, and got back to working *together* instead of against each other.

Practical Conflict-Resolution Techniques for Small Spaces

Conflict resolution in a truck is unique. You can't just "walk away." Instead, you have to learn to handle disagreements quickly, fairly, and without making the truck feel like a battlefield.

1. The "Take a Lap" Rule (Cooling Down Without Storming Off)

Since neither of you can physically leave, the next best thing is taking a mental break.

- ♦ Agree on a short "cooling-off period" after a disagreement.
- ♦ Use that time to breathe, listen to music, or step outside at the next stop instead of saying something you'll regret.
- ♦ After a set time (10–15 minutes), come back and talk with a clearer head.

We've taken many of these "mental laps." One of us puts on noise-canceling headphones, the other takes a short walk at the truck stop. It's amazing what a few minutes of space can do to prevent a blow-up.

2. The "Pilot and Co-Pilot" Approach (Focusing on Solutions, Not Blame)

Think of your relationship like a trucking team. If the pilot (driver) makes a mistake, the co-pilot (co-driver) doesn't scream at them—they work together to fix the issue.

- Instead of pointing fingers, say: "How can we solve this together?"
- Keep the focus on moving forward rather than rehashing old mistakes.

This mindset helped us when we missed a delivery window one time due to miscommunication. Instead of blaming each other, we got on the phone with dispatch, rearranged the drop, and learned how to plan our resets better. It sucked in the moment, but it made us stronger.

3. The "Dispatch Call" Method (Keeping Communication Clear)

Think about how you talk to dispatch or a broker on the phone—straightforward, professional, and focused. You don't scream, you don't drag up last week's problems, and you don't waste time with sarcasm. That same mindset works wonders in conflict resolution with your partner.

- No yelling or name-calling.

- No bringing up five other things from last week.
- No sarcastic "I told you so's."

Stick to the issue at hand. Talk to your spouse the way you'd talk to a teammate—clear, respectful, and solution-focused. It's not about winning the argument—it's about moving forward together.

4. The "What's the Real Problem?" Question

Sometimes, what you're fighting about isn't the real issue.

- Are you arguing about who forgot to fuel up— or is someone actually feeling unappreciated?
- Is it really about who missed the turn—or is exhaustion making tempers flare?

Before arguing, ask yourself: "What's the real problem here?" It helps you get to the root of the issue faster.

A Real-Life Example: Outside Voices, Inside Tension

This past winter, we found ourselves smack in the middle of a snowstorm—one of those stretches where visibility is low, traffic is crawling, and nerves are already on edge. One of us was behind the wheel, carefully navigating the slick highway, while the other was on the phone with a family member.

Now, this family member meant well, but let's just say they're not exactly familiar with trucking—especially winter driving. But that didn't stop them from chiming in with unsolicited advice about what we *should* be doing in the storm. Their commentary quickly turned from concern to critique, and before we knew it, doubt and fear had crept into the cab.

That conversation, though external, managed to create internal conflict. One of us started questioning the driving decisions being made. The other felt undermined. It wasn't about the snow—it was about trust.

After a heated exchange (and some icy silence that matched the weather outside), we had to take a step back. We reminded ourselves of something important: *This is our business. We're the professionals here. We make the decisions.* Not Aunt Linda. Not Cousin Carl. Us.

That moment taught us something big—outside opinions can only shake you if you let them inside. And in a truck, where trust and communication are everything, you've got to protect your partnership from unnecessary interference. We got through that storm by leaning back into each other, not letting anyone else steer our decisions.

Using Humor to Diffuse Tension

Trucking is stressful. Marriage is stressful. But if you can laugh together, you can survive anything.

1. Give the Problem a Funny Name

- Arguing over not paying attention? Call it *The Great Off Ramp Debate of 2016.*
- Arguing over not weighing a load when asked? Call it *The Heavy Weigh Blowout.*
- Giving a silly name to an argument makes it less serious—and easier to move past.

We once had a full-blown spat over adding too much fuel at the truck stop. Now we call it *The Great Fuel Exchange.* Every time we remember it, we laugh instead of argue.

2. Use Inside Jokes as a Reset Button

- Every couple has those goofy little inside jokes. Keep a few in your back pocket to break the tension.
- If you can make your spouse smirk instead of snap, you're already halfway to reconciliation.

3. Play the "Petty Prize" Game

When you realize you're both being stubborn, announce:

"Congratulations! You win the Petty Trophy for today!"

First one to laugh loses the argument (but wins the peace).

4. The "Roadside Reset" Strategy

If an argument is getting heated, one of you can declare a "Roadside Reset."

- ♦ This means: Pause the argument, take a deep breath, and start fresh—as if the fight never happened.
- ♦ It's a way to hit the mental reset button without dragging things out.

When Conflict Teaches You Something

We've had our fair share of cab conflicts, but one in particular taught us something valuable.

During our toughest financial season, we were working under another business owner after our truck engine blew. We were tense, frustrated, and felt trapped in someone else's system. The stress led to more snapping at each other than we care to admit. But instead of letting the pressure divide us, we made a choice: we prayed, we strategized, and we worked together to get out of that situation.

We restructured our finances, cut down on every unnecessary expense, and saved every dime we could. Within a few months, we scraped together the down payment for a new truck. That moment could've broken us, but instead, it became one of our proudest victories— not just as business partners, but as a married team.

Final Thoughts: Rolling Past the Roadblocks

Conflicts are part of any marriage, but in a trucking relationship, you don't have the luxury of distance. That's why learning to resolve disagreements quickly, fairly, and with a sense of humor is essential.

Remember these key takeaways:

♦ Grudges have no place in a truck cab. Resolve issues quickly.

♦ Use practical conflict-resolution techniques. Stay calm, communicate clearly, and focus on solutions.

♦ When in doubt, laugh it out. Humor can turn a bad mood into a bonding moment.

At the end of the day, your marriage is more important than any argument. The road is long, but when you learn to handle conflicts with love, respect, and a little laughter, you'll always be able to ride through the rough patches—together.

CHAPTER 6

COVERING FOR EACH OTHER – STRENGTHS, WEAKNESSES, AND MISTAKES

———— ∞∞∞ ————

There's a silent kind of magic that happens when a trucking couple learns how to *really* have each other's back. Not the Instagram version—where everyone's smiling and coordinating snacks—but the real-life, mile-after-mile, "Hey babe, you forgot to log your yard move" kind of teamwork.

Out here on the road, grace, grit, and shared responsibility matter more than perfection. Because in trucking, as in marriage, you're going to mess up. You'll take the wrong exit, miss a fuel stop, forget to annotate your log, or overestimate your drive time. The difference between a meltdown and a recovery? How well you cover for each other.

This chapter is all about that kind of partnership—the one that admits weaknesses, celebrates strengths, and picks each other up when mistakes happen. Because let's be real: trucking will humble you. But it'll also bond you—if you let it.

Knowing Your Strengths (And Admitting Your Weaknesses)

Every great team works because its members know their roles. You don't see a football quarterback trying to kick field goals—or the wide receiver arguing about who should call the plays. Everyone has a lane. And in trucking, knowing your lane matters just as much.

Maybe one of you is a master trip planner—the kind of person who knows how to calculate ETA, fuel stops, and rest breaks with NASA-level precision. Maybe the other is great at talking to brokers, navigating customer docks, or managing maintenance records. That's not a competition—it's a gift.

How to Figure Out Who Should Do What

Here are some questions we've asked each other (sometimes in a planner, sometimes over a bag of potato chips):

- Who handles stress better in traffic?
- Who is more mechanically inclined?
- Who remembers deadlines and appointments without needing five reminders?
- Who's better with numbers and budgeting?
- Who's more assertive when dealing with brokers or dispatch?
- Who thrives under pressure... and who just needs snacks?

Once you identify your individual strengths, divide responsibilities in a way that plays to them. If one of you can back into a tight dock like a champion but hates paperwork, let them drive while the other handles the documents. You don't *both* have to be great at everything—but together, you should cover all the bases.

And don't just talk about strengths—admit weaknesses too. It's not a sign of failure; it's a sign of maturity. The faster you admit where you struggle, the quicker your partner can support you without judgment.

Real Talk: This Ain't About Ego

Let's say it louder for the people in the back: **There is no room for ego in a team truck.** None. Zilch. Zero.

If one of you insists on doing everything or refuses help out of pride, it's not just bad for the relationship—it's dangerous for the business. Covering for each other only works if both people are willing to be honest and humble.

We've had moments where one of us struggled and didn't want to admit it—only to find out the other *already knew* and was just waiting to help. So don't fake it 'til you make it. Speak up. Trucking is tough enough without trying to impress someone who already sees you at your worst.

Building Backup Systems: Because Mistakes Will Happen

No matter how experienced or careful you are, mistakes will creep in. Fatigue, distractions, pressure… it all adds up. The difference between a rookie move turning into a disaster or a learning experience? **Systems.**

We call these "catch nets." You don't always need them—but when you do, you'll be glad they're there.

1. The Logbook Lifesaver: Double-Checking Each Other's ELDs

We can't tell you how many times one of us has forgotten to annotate something on our logs. No big deal, right? Wrong. That tiny oversight can lead to a violation during an inspection—or worse, mess up your HOS and put your entire schedule at risk.

So, we've created a system: before shutting down or swapping seats, we glance at each other's logs. Did the other person flag their pre-trip? Did they properly mark their off-duty time? Did they add remarks for personal conveyance?

We're not micromanaging—we're protecting each other. That little double-check has saved us from unnecessary violations more than once. If one of us slips, the other catches it. No shame. Just teamwork.

2. The Trip Debrief: Ending Every Shift With Communication

After a driving shift, we don't just hand over the keys and collapse. We take a few minutes to go over trip details:

- ◆ Are there any changes in the route?
- ◆ Did we get special instructions from dispatch?
- ◆ Are there tight turns, tricky docks, or weather updates to know about?

It only takes a few minutes, but it keeps the next driver from being blindsided. It's a small act of consideration that builds trust.

3. The "Mistake Recovery" Plan: Fix It Fast, Fix It Together

Here's a universal trucking truth: if you mess up, the longer you wait to fix it, the worse it gets. Small mistakes can snowball into big problems if you don't catch them early—and fix them fast.

We've had a few of those "oh no" moments ourselves.

There was a time one of us forgot to lock the trailer after getting loaded. We were already several miles down the road before the realization hit. That sinking feeling in your stomach? Yeah—we know it well. We immediately found a safe place to pull over and secured it before anything worse could happen. Could something have gone wrong in those few miles? Absolutely. But thankfully, quick thinking and fast action saved the day.

Another time, we simply didn't secure the load properly. Not on purpose—just distracted and rushing. We were lucky the load didn't shift or get damaged, but it was a major wake-up call. Now we double-check each other's work on high-risk freight. It's not about trust issues—it's about accountability and care.

And of course, who hasn't missed an exit because they were deep in conversation or distracted by the GPS rerouting mid-route? Yep. Been there, done that. It cost us time, miles, and patience. But instead of blaming each other, we worked together to find a safe turnaround and get back on track.

Our Rule: If one of us makes a mistake, we fix it together. No blame. No "I told you so." No sarcasm or side-eye. Just a shared commitment to say, *"Okay, let's make this right."*

Mistakes are inevitable. But staying calm, taking responsibility, and problem-solving as a unit? That's what makes a strong team unstoppable.

Offering Grace: Because You'll Need It Too

It's easy to be gracious when *you* didn't mess up. But the real test is how you respond when your partner drops the ball.

Let's be honest—when you're tired, running late, and someone just forgot to do something important, it's tempting to snap. But biting words don't fix problems—they just deepen wounds.

1. Remember: You'll Be the One Who Messes Up Next

We all have our moments. If your partner just missed a fuel stop or booked a load that didn't pay well, ask yourself how you'd want them to treat *you* in that situation. Probably not with sarcasm or yelling, right?

Give them what you'd want: grace, patience, and maybe a snack.

2. Don't Keep Score

This isn't a competition. If one of you made a mistake last week, and the other messes up this week, that's not a tally system—it's just life. Keeping score leads to resentment. Let it go.

3. Use "We" Language

Instead of saying, "You forgot to check the trailer tires again," say, "How can *we* make sure we check those every time?" It shifts the conversation from blame to solution—and keeps the peace in the cab.

Real-Life Example: Knowing Our Roles and Staying in Our Lane

One of the biggest reasons our partnership works so well is because we've clearly defined our lanes—just like a real business would. We don't compete with each other. We *complement* each other.

One of us is naturally better at keeping track of paperwork, organizing receipts, and managing expenses. That's the administrative department. The other is hands-on with maintenance—keeping an eye on tires, fluids, engine performance, and booking service appointments. That's operations.

We don't step on each other's toes. We don't micromanage. We trust each other to run our department with excellence, and we only jump in when help is requested or needed.

This system didn't just magically appear—we developed it over time through trial, error, and a lot of honest conversations. Now, instead of arguing over who forgot to scan a receipt or who should be booking the next oil change, we stay in our lanes and let each other lead where we're strong.

And when something slips through the cracks? We don't point fingers—we fill in the gap. That's the difference between running a trucking business *as a couple* versus being a couple *in a truck*.

Covering for each other isn't just about avoiding mistakes—it's about *trusting the process, respecting the roles,* and *protecting the partnership.* It's about recognizing that your strengths balance out your spouse's weaknesses, and vice versa.

We've learned that success on the road doesn't come from trying to do everything ourselves. It comes from knowing our lanes—and staying in them.

One of us manages the maintenance, keeping our rig running smooth and safe. The other handles the admin side, making sure every receipt is in order and the business side doesn't miss a beat. Together, we're a well-oiled machine—because we let each other lead in the areas where we shine.

And when we mess up? Because yes, we do—we don't keep score or throw blame. Whether it's forgetting to lock the trailer, missing an exit, or leaving a remark off the logs, we fix it *together,* with grace and humility.

So the next time something slips through the cracks, take a breath. Remind yourselves that you're a team first.

And know this: it's not perfection that makes the partnership work—it's the commitment to cover each other with patience, with trust, and with love.

Because out here, your biggest asset isn't the truck—it's the person in the seat next to you. Stronger together. Every mile.

CHAPTER 7

NOT A COMPETITION –
AVOIDING RIVALRY AND
RESENTMENT

When you're in a truck together 24/7, it's easy—too easy—to slip into a "who does more?" mindset. Who drove the most miles this week? Who took the last difficult dock? Who handled the crazy broker call? Before you know it, your partnership starts to feel like a competition.

And the problem with competition is that someone always has to lose.

Trucking as a couple isn't about proving who's better, tougher, or more productive. It's about building something together—not battling each other over who's working harder. In this chapter, we'll dive into how to avoid rivalry, stay united, and stop keeping score in your relationship and business.

Because in the end, you're not opponents—you're teammates.

Why Comparing Roles or Contributions Leads to Resentment

Keeping score in a marriage—especially in a truck—is a dangerous game. It doesn't bring clarity. It brings tension.

When you focus on proving who does more, you stop appreciating what your partner brings to the table. And since not everything can be easily measured, comparison becomes a trap.

1. Not Everything Can Be Quantified

Sure, you can count miles, weigh loads, and track revenue—but can you measure the emotional toll of being the one who has to deal with dispatch when things go sideways? Or the stress of managing trip plans, insurance deadlines, fuel receipts, and logbook accuracy?

One person might drive the entire night shift while the other handles the business paperwork, health insurance, bookkeeping, agent/broker calls, and planning out the next week's route. That doesn't show up on an odometer—but it matters.

2. Strengths Are Meant to Be Complementary, Not Compared

A good team doesn't have two quarterbacks. A strong marriage doesn't need two identical people. The goal isn't for both of you to do the same things—it's to play to your strengths.

- If one of you is more comfortable on the phone, let them take the broker calls.
- If one of you is a mileage machine and thrives on long-hauls, put them in the seat for the big pushes.
- If one of you is detail-oriented, let them handle logs and compliance.

The point is: you're not rivals. You're running the same race—together.

Real-Life Story: "Buried in Paperwork While One of Us Handles the House"

There was a time when this issue quietly crept into our routine—and it built up before either of us realized it.

After weeks out on the road, we'd finally get home, both drained and ready for some real rest. The first day back was usually simple: unload the truck, hit the shower, crawl into bed. That part was easy.

But the next day? That's where the quiet tension would sneak in.

One of us would start catching up on all the office work—fuel receipts, scanning paperwork, organizing files, checking for missed invoices, reviewing settlements. It was hours of administrative catch-up, and it all had to be done before the next run. The partner in "admin mode" would look up and see the other watching TV or moving around the house, and quietly start to feel overwhelmed. "Why am I buried in all this paperwork while they're relaxing?"

But here's the kicker: the one not doing the admin work wasn't just lounging around.

They were handling everything else—laundry that had piled up from the road, grocery shopping to restock the fridge, fixing things around the house that had gone untouched for weeks. The tasks weren't glamorous or immediately visible, but they were necessary. And in the rush of trying to get everything caught up, both of us missed the truth: **we were both working—just in different ways.**

Neither one of us was slacking. We just weren't communicating.

It took an honest conversation to realize what was happening. The one in the office didn't see the housework as "real work." The one doing the chores didn't understand how mentally draining all the paperwork had become. We both assumed the other had it easier—and that assumption was building quiet resentment.

Now, we're more intentional. We check in. We ask, "Do you need help with anything today?" We list out what needs to be done and divide it—not based on who *usually* does what, but based on what's fair and manageable that day. Most importantly, we recognize that just because something isn't visible doesn't mean it isn't valuable.

We're still refining the balance, but we've learned this: when both partners feel seen and supported, nobody has to keep score.

✅ Checklist: Spotting and Solving Hidden Resentment

Use this list to do a quick check-in with your partner—and yourself—after time on the road or when tension starts to build at home.

👀 Spot the Signs:

- ◆ I've felt like I'm doing more than my share lately.
- ◆ I've caught myself resenting my partner for "relaxing" while I'm still working.
- ◆ I haven't communicated my needs—I've just expected them to notice.
- ◆ I've assumed my partner has it easier without asking what they're managing.

♦ I've been mentally keeping score instead of offering support.

💬 Start the Conversation:

♦ Did I take a moment to ask, "What do you have on your plate today?"

♦ Have we talked about dividing both *house* work and *admin* work fairly?

♦ Have we acknowledged that rest is also a valid and necessary part of recovery?

♦ Did we express appreciation for each other's contributions—seen and unseen?

🫶 Solve It Together:

♦ We made a list of everything that needs to be done this week.

♦ We agreed on who will take what based on time, energy, and skills—not old roles.

♦ We left space in the plan for both rest and unexpected things.

♦ We reminded each other that we're partners—not competitors.

Resentment Starts Small – Spot It Early

Resentment doesn't show up all at once—it creeps in little by little. It starts with a missed thank you. A heavy task load that no one else sees. A sarcastic comment that stings more than it should.

It's the buildup of all the small things left unsaid.

We've learned that if you don't catch resentment early, it turns into something bigger—silence, bitterness, passive-aggressive jabs. All of a sudden, it's not just "you forgot to help with the receipts"—it's "you never help, and I always do everything."

But if you catch it early, you can fix it before it turns toxic.

Here's what we do:

- If we notice we're starting to feel frustrated, we say something early. Calmly. Without blaming.
- We ask each other: "Are we good?" or "Is there anything I can do to support you right now?"
- We listen—really listen—without trying to defend ourselves.

Sometimes, resentment isn't even about the work. It's about not feeling seen. When one of you feels invisible, unappreciated, or taken for granted, that's when the relationship starts to break down.

The fix? Catch the small stuff early. Talk it out. Show appreciation for each other daily. The road is hard enough—don't let unspoken frustrations ride along with you.

How to Stop Keeping Score (And Start Acting Like a Team)

1. Trade "Me vs. You" for "Us"

Instead of:

- ◆ "I drove more than you this week." Try:
- ◆ "We balanced this week well—next time I'll take more rest, and you'll handle the long haul."

Instead of:

- ◆ "You always get the easy shift." Try:
- ◆ "Let's revisit our driving schedule to make sure it feels fair."

A small shift in language goes a long way in maintaining a peaceful rhythm on the road.

2. Celebrate Each Other's Wins

When one of you succeeds, the whole team benefits. So treat every individual win as a shared victory.

Celebrate things like:

- ◆ Getting through a tight backing spot without yelling at each other.
- ◆ Securing a better rate from a broker.
- ◆ Fixing a maintenance issue early before it became a problem.

- Catching a paperwork error and saving a potential fine.

Little wins matter. Celebrate them. Out loud.

3. Ask Instead of Expecting

Most misunderstandings start with unspoken expectations. Just ask.

- "Can you help me sort through the receipts tonight?"
- "Can you take the first shift tomorrow so I can rest?"
- "Would you mind jumping on this broker call? I'm mentally tapped."

You might be surprised how willing your partner is to help—once you simply ask.

Balancing Equality Without Needing Everything to Be the Same

Fairness doesn't mean you each do exactly 50% of everything. It means both of you feel valued and supported in the way that works best for your strengths.

1. Define Your "Departments"

This was a game-changer for us. We created two "departments" for our business:

66

- Operations: driving, maintenance, repairs, fueling, trip routing.
- Administration: receipts, recordkeeping, invoices, compliance, ELD logs.

Each of us leads one department—and we stay in our lanes unless support is needed. It gives us clarity, confidence, and peace of mind.

2. Make Time for Individual Space

Yes, even in a truck, you need space.

That could look like:

- Listening to different music with headphones.
- One person resting in the bunk while the other takes a walk.
- Journaling, gaming, reading, praying— anything that helps you reset as an individual.

You love your partner, but you're still your own person. Honor that.

3. Let Each Other Shine Without Competing

Sometimes, the best way to love your partner is to celebrate their win without making it about you.

- They nailed the perfect blindside back? Say, "That was impressive."
- They caught a mistake on the BOL? Say, "Good eye—thanks for catching that."

♦ They got the rate up an extra hundred bucks? High-five them.

Let your partner shine, and your relationship will shine with them.

Bonus Tips: Practical Ways to Keep Resentment Out of the Cab

1. Weekly Check-Ins

Once a week, take 10–15 minutes to ask each other: "How are we doing?" This gives space to share concerns, offer praise, and course-correct any brewing tension.

2. Use a Shared Task List

Create a running list of admin and driving-related tasks and assign initials or names to them. That way, neither of you feels like you're carrying the invisible weight of remembering everything.

3. Don't Forget Physical Rest

Sometimes resentment comes from exhaustion, not actual disagreement. If one of you is irritable, ask: "Are you just tired?" Before reacting to tension, rule out fatigue.

4. Rotate Roles Occasionally

Even if you've found your lane—admin vs. operations—it doesn't hurt to occasionally switch things up. Let the admin handle driving for a bit if they're up for it, or let the driver sit in on a dispatch call. This builds empathy and appreciation.

5. Laugh Every Day

Seriously—find something to laugh about. A goofy truck stop moment. A mispronounced town name. A dumb inside joke. Laughter kills competition and reconnects you to joy.

Teamwork takes intention, not just time. So keep showing up—not just behind the wheel, but in your commitment to partnership.

Final Thoughts: You Win When Your Partner Wins

At the end of the day, you're not competing—you're co-creating a life. A business. A legacy.

When you stop keeping score, stop trying to "outdo" each other, and start working in sync, your whole operation changes. Suddenly, the load is lighter. The silence becomes peaceful, not punishing. And your partnership deepens in ways that no paycheck can measure.

So next time you feel that rivalry creeping in, take a step back and remember:

- ♦ Your partner is not your competition.
- ♦ Their success is your success.

♦ And your greatest victories will be the ones you *win together.*

CHAPTER 8

ROADSIDE WELLNESS – STAYING HEALTHY TOGETHER

―――――∞∞∞―――――

Trucking is a lifestyle, not just a job. And while the open road offers freedom and adventure, it can also wear you down—physically, mentally, and emotionally. The long hours, inconsistent sleep, fast food, stress, and limited movement? That stuff adds up quickly if you don't make your wellness a daily priority.

But the good news? You're not alone in this. You've got your co-driver—and spouse—riding shotgun.

Being a trucking couple gives you a built-in accountability system. Together, you can encourage healthier habits, help each other course-correct when needed, and look out for signs of fatigue or burnout before they get serious. It's not about perfection. It's about choosing progress and supporting each other every step—or mile—of the way.

In this chapter, we'll dive into:

- ◆ Simple health hacks for eating, sleeping, and staying active on the road.
- ◆ Emotional and mental health check-ins.
- ◆ Building consistent routines and holding each other accountable.
- ◆ Real-life strategies we use to stay well—mind, body, and spirit.

Eating Smarter (Without Going on a Diet)

Truck stop food might be convenient, but it's not exactly built for long-term health. After a while, the fried, salty, carb-loaded meals catch up with you—and not in a good way. We learned that lesson the hard way.

Real-Life Example: Ditching the Truck Stop Buffet

There came a point when we looked at each other and said, "We can't keep eating like this." Burgers. Pizza. Energy drinks. It was quick, easy, and always there—but it left us feeling sluggish, bloated, and just plain off.

So, we started meal prepping at home. Before a trip, we cook full meals—chicken, rice, veggies, soups, or stews—and portion them into microwave-safe containers. We stack them in the truck fridge, and it's as easy as heat and eat. No waiting in line. No post-meal regret.

We also keep healthy snacks on hand: raw veggies, fruit, nuts, and water. We stopped buying sodas and sugary drinks altogether. Cold water stays up front, ready when one of us needs a refresh. And instead of grabbing high-sugar "pick-me-ups," we just stop and rest if we're tired. Simple. Safe. Sustainable.

Sleep: Your Most Important Fuel

Let's be real—sleep is one of the hardest parts of trucking life. Between split shifts, noisy truck stops, and inconsistent schedules, getting good rest can feel like chasing a mirage. But it's non-negotiable.

Sleep affects everything—your safety, your mood, your metabolism, your immune system. So protecting it is part of protecting your partnership and your business.

Our Sleep Habits (and How We Got Better at Them)

We used to push through drowsiness with caffeine or energy drinks. That worked—until it didn't. Eventually, we realized that it was better to take a one to two-hour nap and arrive safe than to risk nodding off and never arriving at all.

Now, if either of us feels that sleepy fog rolling in, we speak up and pull over. Even a short nap makes a big difference. And for deeper rest, we use eye masks, close the back curtains, and noise-canceling headphones when one of us is sleeping while the other drives.

Also: no scrolling in bed. We hold each other accountable for that. When it's time to rest, it's lights out. The phone can wait and goes on silent.

Staying Active in a Small Space

Let's be honest—trucking doesn't exactly scream "fit lifestyle." You're working with tight quarters, long driving hours, unpredictable schedules, and let's not even talk about the temptation to just sit after a long haul. But we've found that staying active doesn't have to mean hitting the gym every day—it just takes a little effort and intention.

We've learned to **make movement a normal part of our day**, even if it's not structured or perfect.

When we park at a truck stop or rest area, we challenge each other to take a walk—even if it's just 5 or 10 minutes. Sometimes one of us will say, "Let's go stretch our legs before we eat," or "Come on, we've been sitting all day— let's move." It's those little nudges that keep us going. We don't always feel like it, but we always feel better afterward.

When time and location allow, we stop at gyms where we have a membership—especially when there's truck parking available. If we've got a few hours to spare on a reset, we'll head in for a light workout, a shower, and just that feeling of doing something good for our bodies. Not every week gives us the opportunity, but when it lines up, we take advantage of it.

And when we're stuck in the truck? We still do what we can. We've gotten into the habit of doing stretch exercises in the cab—neck rolls, shoulder stretches, leg extensions, seated twists. It's nothing fancy, and we don't do it perfectly every day, but even a couple of minutes makes a difference. Sometimes we forget, sure. But we remind each other with a simple "Hey, wanna stretch it out before bed?"

We're not fitness influencers out here—but we are **real people making real choices** to stay well. And those choices matter.

It's not about who can do the most push-ups or having abs of steel. It's about feeling good, having energy, staying limber, and taking care of ourselves so we can keep doing what we love—together.

Mental Health Check-Ins: Keeping Each Other Grounded

This lifestyle wears on your mind just as much as your body. Between the stress of load schedules, dealing with dispatch, long hours, and being away from family, it's easy to feel isolated—even with someone sitting right next to you.

That's why we make mental check-ins part of our routine.

How We Do It

We pay attention to each other's signals. When one of us gets extra quiet or irritable, the other knows it might not be about traffic—it might be something deeper.

We ask:

- "Are you ok?"
- "Need to vent or want space?"
- "What would help you right now?"

Sometimes, we just talk it out. Other times, we play music, listen to a podcast, or even crack jokes to lighten the mood. Our favorite reset? A walk outside and a laugh about something totally unrelated to trucking.

The key is this: your mind needs maintenance too. Don't ignore the check engine light just because you can't see the issue on the outside.

Building Shared Routines and Accountability

The strongest wellness habits we've developed didn't happen overnight—they came from small steps, taken together. Shared routines keep us aligned and make good choices easier to stick to.

Our Daily/Weekly Wellness Habits:

- ◆ We prep meals before trips so we're not tempted by truck stop junk.
- ◆ We both carry water bottles and track our hydration (we even remind each other to sip!).
- ◆ We challenge each other to hit step goals during the day—especially on long-haul runs.
- ◆ We schedule rest days and hold each other to them. No "just one more load" mentality when we're run down.

Accountability doesn't feel like nagging when it's built on mutual care. When one of us reminds the other to take a break, stretch, drink water, or rest—it's not criticism. It's teamwork.

New Section: Preventative Health – Staying Ahead of the Curve

In trucking, most people react to problems—flat tires, late loads, breakdowns. But the best drivers are proactive. Your health should be no different.

We've made it a point to schedule physicals, eye exams, dental appointments, and checkups during our home time. Preventative care keeps small issues from becoming big ones, just like regular truck maintenance does.

We also keep basic vitamins on board, like D3 and B12, etc, and we each take time to walk when we can. That might sound minor—but those grounding moments do more for your well-being than you think.

We don't wait to "feel sick" to take care of ourselves. We build habits that support long-term wellness before there's a problem.

Bonus Tips: Wellness Reminders for Trucking Couples

Here are a few little things we've picked up that make a big difference:

- ◆ **No more energy drinks.** If we're tired, we sleep. Period.
- ◆ **Meal prep = money saved.** Healthier food and fewer impulse purchases.
- ◆ **Park farther.** It adds up. More steps, more movement, more energy.
- ◆ **Pack a first-aid and supplement kit.** Being prepared is peace of mind.

- **Stretch together.** Even 5 minutes helps after a long drive.
- **Share the "why."** Talk about *why* you want to be healthier—so you can be together longer, stronger, and more present in each other's lives.

Final Thoughts: You're Not Just Driving Together—You're Living Well Together

Wellness on the road isn't easy—but it's possible. And when you work as a team, it's sustainable. You don't need a gym membership or a strict routine. You just need intentionality, small changes, and mutual support.

Take care of yourselves. Take care of each other. Rest when you need to, move when you can, and eat like you love your body—not like you're just killing hunger.

Because this isn't just about surviving life on the road. It's about **thriving**—together.

CHAPTER 9

LAUGHING THROUGH THE LANES – KEEPING HUMOR ALIVE

L ife on the road comes with stress, surprises, and plenty of moments that could either make you cry— or make you laugh. The secret to a happy trucking marriage? **Choose laughter every time.**

Laughter is the glue that holds relationships together, especially when you're spending 24/7 in a metal box on wheels. Whether it's an unexpected detour, a miscommunication with dispatch, or a stubborn GPS leading you straight into some strange places, learning to laugh instead of losing your cool can turn an ordinary trip into an unforgettable one.

In this chapter, we'll explore:

♦ Why laughter is essential to marriage and mental health

♦ Funny stories from the road (including our own favorites!)

♦ How to turn frustrating moments into comedy

♦ How humor helps you de-escalate conflict

♦ Fun habits and ideas to keep joy alive in your trucking life

Laughter Is a Stress Buster on Wheels

Let's face it—trucking can be downright ridiculous sometimes. The long hours, the clueless four-wheelers, the "surprise" construction zones, or that one shipper who *always* takes six hours to load you—this life comes with stress baked in.

But laughter? Laughter is like a reset button. It turns pressure into perspective.

Real-Life Example: "God Is Kissing Our Forehead Today"

One night after a frustrating day of delays, traffic, and rain, we rolled into a packed truck stop. We were mentally done. Exhausted. Ready to find a field and just lay down somewhere.

Just as we were about to give up, a driver pulled out of the *perfect* spot—front row, near the store, easy back-in.

Without missing a beat, one of us shouted, "God is kissing our forehead today!" We both laughed so hard it broke the tension of the entire day. That moment became a phrase we still use: when something unexpectedly good happens, we know God's looking out for us.

Small Spaces, Big Laughs

When you live in tight quarters, everything feels magnified. If your partner chews too loud, folds laundry the "wrong" way, or sings off-key to old-school R&B—it can feel like nails on a chalkboard.

But here's what we've learned: the key to surviving (and thriving) in a small space isn't silence—it's laughter.

- ◆ One of us always misplaces stuff, so we created an official "Give it a Home Place" in the cab. We make it a habit of placing it in the same place we retrieved it from.
- ◆ When the "hangry" attitude kicks in, the other tosses over a granola bar or available snack from the snack basket and says, "Eat this before we both regret it."
- ◆ One of us gives running commentary to bad drivers who turn corners too wide or too fast. "That four-wheeler came around that corner

like they stole something!". Or, "They shaved that corner, didn't they?"

Real-Life Story: The Horn Incident

We once parked at a truck stop, people-watching (like truckers do). A fellow driver nearby was clearly exhausted. His eyes were halfway closed, nodding off right there in his seat.

Next thing you know—*BEEEEEP!* His head dropped onto the horn. He jumped like someone set off fireworks inside his cab. He sat up so fast, confused and wide-eyed like a deer staring in headlights.

We still laugh about it to this day. Because we remember the goofy look he had on his face when his head hit the steering wheel.

It's those moments—real, raw, human—that become the glue that holds you together.

The Cab Chronicles: Corny Lines, Crazy Drivers, and Comedy Gold

Bad days happen. But when you've got each other, a windshield view of the world, and a sense of humor, every day brings material for your own private comedy show.

1. Corny Pickup Line Hour

One of our favorite games is seeing who can come up with the cheesiest, most cringe-worthy pickup line on the spot. The goal? Make the other person laugh, groan, or both. Bonus points if it's trucking-themed.

- ♦ "Are you a weigh station? Because you just made me pull over."
- ♦ "Baby, if loving you was a DOT regulation, I'd never be out of compliance."
- ♦ "You must be my logbook… because I can't stop thinking about you."

Even on the longest, roughest days, these lines get us smiling—and keep the flirtation alive.

2. Comedians in a Freightliner

Sometimes we put on a clean comedy special while driving and end up laughing so hard we're crying. It's like therapy on wheels. There's nothing better than busting up over jokes that don't involve dispatch, delays, or diesel prices (well… maybe just a few jokes about diesel prices).

Laughter on the move has helped us decompress during some seriously stressful hauls. The road still rolls on, but suddenly it feels a whole lot lighter.

3. Highway Hilarity: People Are Wild

If you've ever driven a truck, you've seen things. And if you've *team-driven*, you've had someone to *witness* those things with.

Like the time we watched a guy cut across three lanes of traffic, the grassy median, and two more lanes of oncoming traffic—all just to get into a fast food drive-thru. We were stunned. It was like watching a NASCAR pit stop directed by someone with zero GPS signal and a craving for fries.

We looked at each other and said, "That man needed that burger like his life depended on it."

And honestly? Maybe it did.

We don't take notes for a Netflix comedy special—we just live our life. The characters, the chaos, the corny love? It's all right there in the cab.

So if you're rolling through a rough day, flip the mental channel. Find the humor. Be the comic relief. Because laughter isn't just how we cope—it's how we connect.

The "Did That Just Happen?" Moments

Some moments in trucking are so random, so ridiculous, so *uniquely us*, that they go from normal to unhinged in less than ten seconds. We call these our "Did That Just Happen?" moments—the stuff that starts off ordinary and takes a sharp left turn into chaos or comedy.

Let's just say… we've had more than a few.

1. Silly Songs & Crazy Accents

Sometimes, after a long day on the road, we don't want to talk logistics, routing, or anything remotely productive. Instead? We burst into song—but not just any song.

We'll sing like a country singer with a mouthful of marshmallows, or do an entire ballad in an over-the-top British accent. One of us once sang "I Will Always Love You" like Kermit the Frog during a mountain descent, and we both laughed so hard the truck was practically vibrating from the wheezing.

It's like karaoke meets truck stop therapy. It resets the mood every time.

2. Hazmat Humor

Then there are the moments where one of us forgets we're not *entirely* alone.

Like the time one of us bent over to grab something off the floor… directly in front of the other's face. No warning. No apology. Just full, unexpected view.

The reaction? A deadpan delivery:

"Wow… should I put a hazmat placard on that?"

We were crying from laughter for ten solid minutes. Now, every time someone leans over, the other pretends to reach for the dangerous placard label.

It's ridiculous. It's childish. It's *exactly* what we need.

3. The Escalation is the Entertainment

These are the moments that don't make sense to anyone else—but they're gold to us. The stuff you don't plan. You don't script. It just happens when you're comfortable enough with your partner to be completely weird and absolutely yourself.

Whether we're:

- ♦ Having a dance battle while fueling,
- ♦ Doing fake movie trailer voiceovers about our day ("In a world where drivers were *out of hours...*"),
- ♦ Or trying to one-up each other's terrible puns until someone gives up laughing—

We lean into the weird. Because weird keeps the road fun, and laughter keeps the love strong.

Lighthearted Habits That Keep You Laughing: The "Remember That One Time?" Recap

We've learned that one of the best ways to keep joy in our relationship is by **retelling our funniest memories.** No fancy rituals, no deep therapy sessions—just two people, rolling down the road, laughing over things that once had us stunned, speechless, or straight-up bent over wheezing.

We call it our **"Remember that one time..." recap.** And we pull it out any time the cab feels a little heavy, the day gets long, or we just need a reminder that we've seen—and survived—it all.

🚚 "Remember that one time we were driving down I-17 in Flagstaff?"

That descent is no joke—18 miles of steep grade that'll eat your brakes alive if you don't respect it.

We were doing everything right: pacing ourselves, engine braking, keeping it slow and safe. Then, out of nowhere, here comes a truck *blazing* down the mountain like it was auditioning for an action movie.

His brakes were smoking. His eyes were wide. His face said, *"This was not the plan."*

We caught up with him at the rest area halfway down. He was parked with the door open, smoke still rolling out from under the trailer. No one spoke—we all just exchanged that universal trucker look: *"Been there, brother. Been there."*

We still laugh about the expression on his face like, *"Lord, if you get me through this one, I promise I'll never take that hill hot again."*

👍 "Remember that one time at the truck stop bathroom…"

This one's legendary in our book.

One of us went into a stall, got comfortable, then realized—too late—there was **no toilet paper.** None in the stall. None on standby. And no bag on the door saying it was out.

Panic? No. This was the *trucking community*, and the stall neighbors had our back.

From the next stall over came a quiet voice:

"You good? Need a square?"

Not only did someone pass over a few pieces—folded neatly like a peace offering—but another driver jumped in with, "I got napkins if y'all need a support team."

Drivers were rationing toilet paper like it was the apocalypse. We were cracking up the whole time. It was a terrible situation turned wholesome, awkward, and hilarious—one of those weird, beautiful bonding moments you only get on the road.

"Remember that one time we saw a guy risk it all for a burger?"

We were driving through town, just cruising down the highway, when this car—out of nowhere—**cut across ALL lanes of traffic**, the grassy median, and the opposing lanes just to whip into a fast-food parking lot.

No signal. No hesitation. Just pure, greasy determination.

He didn't even slow down. Just *boom*, across the highway like he had a personal invitation from the drive-thru speaker.

We were speechless. Then we both busted out laughing like, "That man needed those fries like his life depended on it."

Now whenever one of us is hungry and getting snappy, the other says, "Don't make me do a fast-food emergency exit," and we both crack up.

These are the stories that keep us smiling on hard days. They're not written in a journal or recorded in some logbook—but they live in our conversations, always ready to come back when we need a good laugh.

Humor doesn't have to be scripted. Sometimes it just needs to be remembered.

Keep a Laugh Log – The Rolling Comedy Journal

We keep a "Laugh Log" in the notes app on our phone—a running list of things that had us wheezing, wiping tears, and sometimes pulling over to recover. It's not fancy, and it's definitely not filtered. But on tough days, all we have to do is scroll, and the laughter comes back instantly.

Here are just a few gems from our rolling comedy archive:

- **"Used Spouse for Sale – Limited Warranty, No Returns, Final Sale."** Written after one of us acted up in the grocery store.

- **"You can't fix stupid, but you can honk at it."** What we say every time a four-wheeler cuts us off, slams on the brakes, and acts surprised we can't stop in two feet.

- **"Rest Stop Runway: Man in a pink tutu coming out of the woods, winking at drivers."** We thought we were hallucinating. One driver was so distracted, he almost rear-ended the truck in front of him. The man had confidence. We gave him a mental 10 out of 10 for boldness and costume choice.

We add to the Laugh Log every week. Sometimes it's just a line. Sometimes it's a full story. But it always reminds us why we love this life—and why we love doing it together.

Because in trucking, you've got to log more than just miles. You've got to log the moments that make it all worth it.

Final Thoughts: Let Joy Ride Shotgun

The truth is, this lifestyle will test you. Not once, not twice, but constantly. The key to staying connected, sane, and happily married in a eight foot rolling box is choosing joy—daily.

♦ Laugh when the truck wash line is 15 trucks deep.

♦ Laugh when your GPS loses signal in the middle of nowhere.

♦ Laugh when your sandwich falls upside down... again use laughter turns breakdowns into bonding, delays into memories, and this unpredictable life into an unforgettable adventure.

So go ahead—tell the joke. Do the voice. Make the ridiculous comment. Crack up at the dumbest meme. And when in doubt, remember this:

The most important load you carry isn't in the trailer—it's in your heart.

CHAPTER 10

REFLECTING ON THE ROAD BEHIND AND THE JOURNEY AHEAD

The odometer may keep turning, but every now and then, you've got to pause, look back, and appreciate how far you've come. As we bring this book—and this chapter of our journey—to a close, we're filled with gratitude for the miles we've traveled, both on the road and in our relationship.

When we first climbed into a truck together, we didn't realize we were signing up for the ultimate crash course in marriage, business, logistics, patience, forgiveness, and personal growth. We thought we were just teaming up to run loads and make money. We didn't know we'd also be learning how to navigate breakdowns—mechanical and emotional—and how to become not just co-drivers, but co-leaders, co-creators, and co-survivors of this wild ride called life on 18 wheels.

And yet, here we are. Stronger. Closer. Wiser. Definitely more graying. And definitely more grateful.

The Road Was Our Teacher

We say this often: trucking didn't just test us—it taught us. The road has a way of humbling you while building you up. And if you're paying attention, every mile brings a lesson.

We learned that **love doesn't need four walls**. It can survive—and thrive—inside an 8-foot-wide rolling metal box as long as it's built on respect, patience, and shared purpose.

In Chapter 1, we talked about how being married on the move is about learning to **laugh in the chaos**. And that's still one of our top survival skills. When your relationship lives between truck stops and tire blowouts, humor becomes holy. Laughter has carried us through moments when GPS rerouted us down a wrong road trail in a state we didn't mean to cross into, when one of us wanted to abandon the truck mid-hill, and when fingers and "words" from angry motorists became the soundtrack to our day.

But we also learned the seriousness of the job—especially in Chapter 3, where we dove into **Mind Over Miles**. There were days we felt like giving up. Days when our motivation ran out before our hours of service did. But our commitment to each other—and to a bigger purpose—kept us rolling. We discovered the power of praying together, of encouraging each other when one of us hit a wall, and of holding tight to our "why" when the road ahead felt impossible.

Real Growth Happens in Real Conflict

No couple spends this much time in a cab together without a few... *heated discussions*. In Chapter 5, we got honest about **cab conflicts**. We shared how even well-meaning outside voices (hello, Aunt Linda in the snowstorm) can stir up fear and doubt between you if you're not grounded in trust.

We learned that **conflict is inevitable, but damage is optional**. That even when we mess up—like booking a terrible load, missing an exit, or forgetting to lock the trailer—it's not about pointing fingers. It's about solving problems together, offering grace, and pressing reset.

Let's be real: the truck doesn't offer a whole lot of room to stew in silence. So, we had to learn how to fight fair, speak up early, and forgive fast. And when we couldn't find the words, sometimes a shared laugh or a silly inside joke worked better than any therapy session.

Our Hardest Season—And Our Biggest Breakthrough

You've read the story already, but it bears repeating—because it changed everything.

When our truck engine blew, everything stopped. For a while, so did we. We were faced with decisions we never thought we'd have to make. Work under someone else? Start over? Tighten our budget like never before? It was one of the most humbling seasons of our lives.

But it was also where we saw the true strength of our partnership.

We prayed. We planned. We sacrificed. And we hustled—smart. That moment taught us more than any business seminar ever could: that **shared goals turn setbacks into stepping stones**. That unity under pressure produces diamonds. And that the truck might've been out of commission, but we weren't.

Eventually, we saved enough to get back into our own truck. And let us tell you: that first run back on our own terms felt like the sweetest victory of our entire career.

Covering for Each Other—Then and Always

In Chapter 6, we talked about what it means to **cover for each other**. It's not just about taking turns or swapping driving shifts. It's about paying attention. It's seeing when your partner is drained, distracted, or in need—and stepping in without being asked.

We've developed systems: double-checking logs, ending shifts with quick recaps, having pre-trip "briefings" over breakfast burritos. But more than systems, we've built trust. Because in this lifestyle, mistakes aren't just costly—they can be dangerous. Knowing we've got each other's back isn't just comforting. It's essential.

And when we mess up? Because we do—it's not about keeping score. It's about helping each other recover, learn, and move forward.

You Can't Compete and Connect at the Same Time

We used to silently compare who drove more miles, who dealt with more stress, or who had the harder day. But Chapter 7 was a turning point—the chapter where we decided to stop competing and start celebrating each other.

We realized that **success doesn't look the same for both of us.** One of us might be buried in admin work while the other's tackling grocery runs and laundry. One might be hauling the heavy night shifts while the other's fighting with the ELD system or planning the next load. Both matter.

Now, we check in more intentionally. We ask, "Do you need help with anything today?" We've stopped assuming—and started asking. And it's transformed our teamwork.

Wellness on the Road Isn't Optional

Chapter 8 reminded us that **taking care of our bodies is how we take care of our business and our bond.** We're not perfect—there were plenty of weeks when fast food and fatigue were our only companions— but we're learning. We prep meals, hold each other accountable, and speak up when we see the other slipping into burnout.

Staying healthy isn't just about us individually—it's about staying strong as a unit. If one person falls apart, the whole team slows down. So we prioritize rest, make space for silence, and give grace for recovery.

Looking Ahead: The Journey Still Matters

We don't know where the road will take us next. Maybe one day we'll park the truck for good and step into a new season—writing, mentoring, or maybe just enjoying a little peace and quiet. But whether we're in the cab or watching sunsets from a porch swing, we know this:

We built something incredible together.

Not just a business. Not just a lifestyle. But a **legacy.**

And if we had to do it all again—even the engine failures, the snowstorms, the missed exits, and the low-paying loads—we would. Because this journey grew us. It connected us. And it gave us stories we'll tell for the rest of our lives.

To Every Trucking Couple Out There

If you've made it this far in the book, you're part of our family now. Whether you're a few months in or a few million miles deep, we hope you see yourselves in these pages.

You are not alone.

Your story matters.

Your partnership matters.

The road is hard—but so are you.

So keep driving. Keep laughing. Keep resetting when needed. Keep praying when it gets tough. And above all, keep choosing each other—mile after mile.

Because the most important load you'll ever carry is the one sitting next to you in that passenger seat or in the sleeper.

Final Thoughts: This Isn't the End—Just the Next Mile Marker

If you've made it this far, thank you—for sticking with us through the long haul, for laughing at our stories, and for giving us the chance to share what life on 18 wheels really looks like when you're doing it with your partner.

Maybe you read this book curled up in the bunk between loads. Maybe you listened to chapters together during a long stretch across I-80. However and wherever you found time, we hope something in these pages helped you breathe a little deeper, laugh a little louder, or look at your partner with fresh eyes—even if they just missed the exit again.

We wrote this book not because we've got it all figured out, but because we're still learning, too. Every load, every season, every challenge teaches us something new about marriage, about business, and about ourselves. And what we've learned is this: you never really "arrive." You just keep hitting mile markers—moments where you stop, reflect, reset, and keep rolling.

Some days will be smooth and sunny; others will be filled with brake checks, blown tires, and blown tempers. But through it all, you get to do this with your best friend. That's the part people don't always see. Not just the freight or the fuel or the miles—but the faith, the grit, the grace, and the love that keep the wheels turning.

You've learned that roles matter, but teamwork matters more. That communication is everything. That conflict doesn't have to be catastrophic. That there's power in knowing your strengths—and peace in letting go of comparison. You've seen what happens when two people choose to build something together, even when the road gets bumpy.

And now?

Now it's your turn to keep writing the story—mile by mile, chapter by chapter.

At the end of the day, trucking together is more than a job—it's a calling, a commitment, and a wild ride you choose to take side by side. Through late-night runs, engine trouble, unexpected detours, and quiet sunsets over the dash, you've learned how to drive freight and grow a future—together. You've learned that success doesn't come from perfection, but from showing up for each other mile after mile, load after load, conversation after conversation. Whether you're sharing a laugh after a wrong turn or navigating your way through a tough season, remember: your greatest asset isn't your GPS, your logbook, or even your hustle—it's the person riding shotgun. So here's to the couples on 18 wheels—loving fiercely, living freely, and proving every day that home isn't a place... it's a partnership.

End-of-the-Road Reflection Questions

Want to take a moment to pause together? Use these questions to reflect at the end of your week, month, or even at the end of a haul:

1. What was one moment this week that made you laugh?
2. What's one thing your partner did recently that you appreciate?
3. What challenge did you overcome together that made you stronger?
4. How have you grown—individually and as a couple—since you started driving together?
5. What's one memory from the road that you want to tell your grandkids?

Journaling & Reflection: Your Turn to Look Back (and Ahead)

Use these questions to reflect individually or with your partner. Whether you're just starting out or have a million miles behind you, take time to pause and check-in. Your story matters.

1. How have we grown as individuals—and as a couple—since we started trucking together?
2. What challenges nearly broke us, and what helped us overcome them?
3. In what ways are we stronger now than when we first started this journey?

4. What are our shared goals for the next year? Five years?

5. Are there any unspoken resentments or roles that need to be revisited in our partnership?

6. What makes us laugh the hardest on the road— and how can we create more of those moments?

7. What's one thing I can do this week to better support my co-driver—both as a business partner and a spouse?

8. What is our "why"? What vision fuels us when the days get hard?

Take your time with these. Journal your answers. Talk them out on the next long stretch. Let them guide your next steps—not just in your business, but in your bond.

And remember: the road may be long, but the journey is richer when you roll through it together.

We're rooting for you. Always.

A WORD FROM THE AUTHORS

With over 40 years of combined experience in the trucking industry, we've come to understand that success isn't just about miles—it's about mindset. We've learned that staying committed, focused, and purpose-driven is what truly keeps the wheels turning.

This journey has taught us to think creatively, adapt quickly, and tackle challenges head-on. We've grown by being solution-minded and stepping out of the "this is how it's always been done" mentality. And that's where the real transformation began.

So if you're standing at the edge of a decision or feeling stuck in your routine, we invite you to lean into growth. **Give yourself permission to dream bigger, plan smarter, and move forward boldly.** The road ahead is full of opportunity—and you're more than capable of navigating it.

– Robert & Sharon Porter

ABOUT THE AUTHORS

Robert and **Sharon Porter** are a husband-and-wife trucking team with over four decades of combined experience in the transportation industry. What began as a shared curiosity and love for the open road became a thriving business and an even stronger partnership—on and off the road. As co-owners, co-drivers, and co-dreamers, they've learned how to navigate not only the highways of America, but the winding roads of marriage, entrepreneurship, and faith.

Sharon, a licensed driver since 1994, was inspired early on by her father's long career in trucking and the freedom it represented. She brings a fierce determination, an unshakable belief in purpose, and a deep well of spiritual strength to their business and their life. Robert, with over 30 years of experience, was captivated as a child by the romantic idea of life on the road, thanks to the television show *Moving On*. That inspiration became a lifelong calling, driven by discipline, mentorship, and a love for people.

Together, they've faced engine failures, financial setbacks, cab conflicts, and moments of uncertainty—but through it all, they've chosen unity over blame, vision over fear, and grace over ego. Their journey is one of faith, forgiveness, and a whole lot of laughter, and this book is their love letter to every couple learning how to do life—and business—as a team.

They currently run their own trucking business, create content for aspiring drivers and couples, and mentor others on how to thrive behind the wheel without losing sight of what matters most. When they're not rolling down the highway, you'll find them somewhere quiet, fishing pole in hand or journal on the dash, planning their next adventure together.

Stay Connected – Share Your Story With Us

—————⧜⧜⧜—————

We wrote this book because we know how lonely, wild, and beautiful life on the road can be—and we believe every trucking couple has a story worth telling.

If you found encouragement, humor, or a moment that made you nod in agreement, we'd love to hear about it. Tell us what made you laugh. Share the stories that hit home. Let us know which chapter you read aloud to your co-driver while sitting at a rest stop.

You can find us on social media—we're always down for a chat, a laugh, or a virtual fist bump after a long haul.

📱 **Connect with us:**

- Instagram: @LoveOn18Wheels
- Facebook: Love On 18 Wheels – The Book
- TikTok: @TruckinTogether
- Email: hello@loveon18wheels.com

www.ingramcontent.com/pod-product-compliance
Lightning Source LLC
LaVergne TN
LVHW011336080426
835513LV00006B/375